# MacNab

## by Jason MacNab

Lang**Syne**

**PUBLISHING**

WRITING *to* REMEMBER

**LangSyne**

**PUBLISHING**

WRITING *to* REMEMBER

Vineyard Business Centre,
Pathhead, Midlothian EH37 5XP
Tel: 01875 321 203 Fax: 01875 321 233
E-mail: info@lang-syne.co.uk
www.langsyneshop.co.uk

Design by Dorothy Meikle
Printed by Montgomery Litho, Glasgow
© Lang Syne Publishers Ltd 2011

ISBN 978-1-85217-086-8

# MacNab

**SEPT NAMES INCLUDE:**
Abbott
Cleland
Dewar
Gilfillan
Gillan
Maclellan
MacNair

# MacNab

**MOTTO:**
Let all fear be absent.

**CREST:**
The Head of a Savage.

**PLANT BADGE:**
Stone bramble.

**TERRITORY:**
Perthshire.

*Chapter one:*

# The origins of the clan system

by Rennie McOwan

**The original Scottish clans of the Highlands and the great families of the Lowlands and Borders were gatherings of families, relatives, allies and neighbours for mutual protection against rivals or invaders.**

Scotland experienced invasion from the Vikings, the Romans and English armies from the south. The Norman invasion of what is now England also had an influence on land-holding in Scotland. Some of these invaders stayed on and in time became 'Scottish'.

The word clan derives from the Gaelic language term 'clann', meaning children, and it was first used many centuries ago as communities were formed around tribal lands in glens and mountain fastnesses.

The format of clans changed over the centuries, but at its best the chief and his family held the land on behalf of all, like trustees, and the ordinary clansmen and women believed they had a blood relationship with the founder of their clan.

There were two way duties and obligations. An inadequate chief could be deposed and replaced by someone of greater ability.

Clan people had an immense pride in race. Their relationship with the chief was like adult children to a father and they had a real dignity.

The concept of clanship is very old and a more feudal notion of authority gradually crept in.

Pictland, for instance, was divided into seven principalities ruled by feudal leaders who were the strongest and most charismatic leaders of their particular groups.

By the sixth century the 'British' kingdoms of Strathclyde, Lothian and Celtic Dalriada (Argyll) had emerged and Scotland, as one nation, began to take shape in the time of King Kenneth MacAlpin.

Some chiefs claimed descent from

ancient kings which may not have been accurate in every case.

By the twelfth and thirteenth centuries the clans and families were more strongly brought under the central control of Scottish monarchs.

Lands were awarded and administered more and more under royal favour, yet the power of the area clan chiefs was still very great.

The long wars to ensure Scotland's independence against the expansionist ideas of English monarchs extended the influence of some clans and reduced the lands of others.

Those who supported Scotland's greatest king, Robert the Bruce, were awarded the territories of the families who had opposed his claim to the Scottish throne.

In the Scottish Borders country - the notorious Debatable Lands - the great families built up a ferocious reputation for providing war-like men accustomed to raiding into England and occasionally fighting one another.

Chiefs had the power to dispense justice

and to confiscate lands and clan warfare produced a society where martial virtues - courage, hardiness, tenacity - were greatly admired.

Gradually the relationship between the clans and the Crown became strained as Scottish monarchs became more orientated to life in the Lowlands and, on occasion, towards England.

The Highland clans spoke a different language, Gaelic, whereas the language of Lowland Scotland and the court was Scots and in more modern times, English.

Highlanders dressed differently, had different customs, and their wild mountain land sometimes seemed almost foreign to people living in the Lowlands.

It must be emphasised that Gaelic culture was very rich and story-telling, poetry, piping, the clarsach (harp) and other music all flourished and were greatly respected.

Highland culture was different from other parts of Scotland but it was not inferior or less sophisticated.

Central Government, whether in London

*"The spirit of the clan means much
to thousands of people"*

or Edinburgh, sometimes saw the Gaelic clans as a challenge to their authority and some sent expeditions into the Highlands and west to crush the power of the Lords of the Isles.

Nevertheless, when the eighteenth century Jacobite Risings came along the cause of the Stuarts was mainly supported by Highland clans.

The word Jacobite comes from the Latin for James - Jacobus. The Jacobites wanted to restore the exiled Stuarts to the throne of Britain.

The monarchies of Scotland and England became one in 1603 when King James VI of Scotland (1st of England) gained the English throne after Queen Elizabeth died.

The Union of Parliaments of Scotland and England, the Treaty of Union, took place in 1707.

Some Highland clans, of course, and Lowland families opposed the Jacobites and supported the incoming Hanoverians.

After the Jacobite cause finally went down at Culloden in 1746 a kind of ethnic cleansing took place. The power of the chiefs was curtailed.  Tartan and the pipes were banned in law.

Many emigrated, some because they wanted to, some because they were evicted by force. In addition, many Highlanders left for the cities of the south to seek work.

Many of the clan lands became home to sheep and deer shooting estates.

But the warlike traditions of the clans and the great Lowland and Border families lived on, with their descendants fighting bravely for freedom in two world wars.

Remember the men from whence you came, says the Gaelic proverb, and to that could be added the role of many heroic women.

The spirit of the clan, of having roots, whether Highland or Lowland, means much to thousands of people.

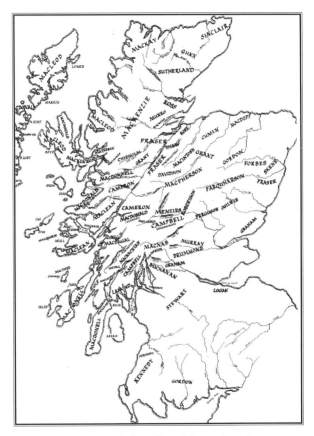

*A map of the clans' homelands*

*Chapter two:*

# War and betrayal

**The MacNabs have won fame out of all proportion to their size as a clan.**

They were responsible for one of the most daring incidents in the history of clan warfare; they produced perhaps the most colourful chief ever seen in the Highlands; and they were involved in a famous, not to say notorious, attempt to reproduce the old feudal system in the New World of the Canadian wilderness.

The homeland for the Clan MacNab is centred on the small Perthshire town of Killin and stretches from there up Glen Dochart and along the south side of Loch Tay. But the great symbol of the MacNab's identity, the one territory to survive all the clan's startling vicissitudes, is the small island of Inchbuie on the River Dochart, the beautiful, yellow isle of Scots pine beeches and sycamores where the chiefs and their kinsmen have been buried

since the name and race of MacNab was
formed.

This means since the 12th or 13th centu-
ry, for at about that time lived the son of the Abbot
MacAnaba who gave his title to the clan. This
does not imply that the race springs illegitimately
from a clerical indiscretion.

The abbots of the old Celtic church were
secular and hereditary great lords rather than
cloistered celibates, leaders of their people in war
as often as in prayer. The MacNabs' originators
were Abbots of St. Fillan's monastery near Loch
Earn and were probably more junior members of
the MacGregor family since we know that in 1140
Sir John MacGregor was Abbot of St. Fillan's and
that the MacNabs are part of the great Gaelic
breed descended from the ancient Princes of
Dalriada and Ulster of which the MacGregors are
the main modern stem.

St. Fillan himself, who died in 703, was a
Prince of this Royal house; and the importance of
the blood is confirmed by the fact that, when the
MacNabs held the diocese, it was equal with the

neighbouring Earldoms of Atholl and Monteith and was therefore second in rank only to the Royal blood of Scotland itself; and so, when the Celtic Church was reformed in the Roman model and the MacNabs chose to become out and out secular lords rather than retire into monasteries, it was natural that they should be granted the Barony of Glen Dochart created for them from their own monastery clans.

This happened at the time of the death of Alexander the Third in 1286, an event which precipitated the War of Independence with England and brought the MacNabs their firstserious setback

The two main claims to the throne came from the Balliols of Galloway and the Bruces of Annandale. The Bruces were backed by most of southern Scotland and the Central Highlands, the Balliols supported by the East Coast and Western clans. The MacNabs automatically followed the MacDougalls of Lorne into the Balliol camp and this meant into the English camp. Both Edward I and his son tried to use the Balliols to exert their own authority over Scotland. Because of this, many of the MacNabs' enemies tried to represent them as traitors, forgetting that Scotland was genuinely split over the succession.

Whatever the rights and wrongs, the MacNabs certainly suffered by choosing what turned out to be the losing side. Though MacDougall defeated Robert Bruce at Dalrigg, the allies of the English went down with them at Bannockburn.

And the MacNabs were soon deprived of their land and driven back onto Inchbuie, then, as later, their very last resort in time of trouble.

They also probably suffered the loss of their chief and his two sons at this time for it is said that the MacNabs were the three men killed by King Robert when they tried to ambush him after his defeat at Dalrigg. This story is told in Barbour's epic poem 'The Bruce' and since he describes the men in question as the mightiest men of the West, and the MacNabs were already known for their stature and strength, it is very possible that they were the clan involved. If so, their might did them little good on this occasion because, when they sprang out in front of him in a narrow path above a river valley, Bruce charged them full tilt, knocking one of the sons into the valley below. The other two tried to pull him to the ground by clinging to his horse but Bruce cut one of them at the neck and severed the arm of the other which was left still grasping his bridle as he rode off to safety.

The clan soon recovered from these set-backs and worked their way into the favour of King David Bruce who in 1336 gave a new charter for Glen Dochart to Gilbert MacNab, the first fully documented chief of his people. There now followed 300 years of feuding as the MacNabs fought with the MacGregors and with their own sept, the Dewars.

*Chapter three:*

# Massacre at Loch Earn

**The Earls of Breadalbane looked on coldly, forever scheming to take advantage of these feuds by moving into their rivals' land. The first performance of what soon became a familiar play was acted at the beginning of the 15th century when the MacNabs and MacGregors fought each other to a bloody draw at Crianlarich, the two chiefs only calling a halt after giving each other serious injuries in a personal combat.**

Immediately, the Glen Orchy Campbells moved in. They invaded the territories of both clans and sought to have them declared forfeit at Edinburgh. The MacGregors, accepting the challenge, took to the hills. The MacNabs, more wisely perhaps, gave up some land in order to keep others and soon staged a recovery, receiving new estates in Royal Charters of 1487 and 1502. In this latter year, too, we find evidence of a continuing connection with St. Fillan for another charter of that date from the Prior of the monastery at Perth grants the MacNab chief the revenue of some crofts at Killin in exchange for three pounds of wax yearly in honour of the Blessed Virgin and St. Fillan for the increase of the saint's light before his image, 'one pound thereof at the feast of St. Fillan in summer and another at the feast of St. Fillan in winter'. It can be seen from this that the Scots were not very good arithmeticians in those days.

What they were good at was fighting! And at about the same time as this, St. Fillan cropped up again as the cause of a feud between the MacNabs and the Dewars. He had left to his monastery two important relics, a crozier and a bell of which the MacNabs became hereditary custodians until the 13th century. Then the crozier somehow passed into the hands of the Dewars who afterwards used it as a symbol of their independence. The relics were also important as entitling the holders to a place of honour at the Coronations of Scottish kings. So in 1510 the

MacNabs launched an armed foray to recover the
crozier from the Dewars' territory in upper Glen
Dochart. There was another inconclusive fight
which was again exploited by the Campbells who
waited until the battle was over then declared
themselves allies of the Dewars and marched into
the MacNabs estate.

The Campbells' infiltration was greatly
facilitated by the financial responsibility of the
sixth MacNab Chief, Finlay the Mortgager, who
fell for the old Campbell ploy of buying up debts
of their rivals and lost control of his estates to such
an extent that by 1580 Glen Orchy was telling
King James that he had 'conquested the
MacNab's whole landis'. This claim was never
accepted by the MacNabs but they were obvious-
ly in deep trouble at the time for a Crown investi-
gation into the state of the Western clans lists them
amongst those which had been broken for punishment of theft, oppression and blackmail. Again,
though the recovery was swift, the next chief,
also Finlay, made the best of a bad job by marry-
ing Campbell of Glen Orchy's daughter and

fathering a dozen sons as if to prove his sincerity in making peace with the old enemy.

In 1610 two hundred Campbells, MacNabs and MacDonalds defeated a great force of MacGregors, securing the Lordship of Breadalbane for Glen Orchy and lands for MacNab. Once again the MacNabs were sitting pretty and two years later they sprang into national fame by their extermination of local rivals, the MacNeishes of Loch Earn.

Finlay MacNab's twelve sons continued the family traditions of gigantism and ferocity. It was said that even the youngest and smallest of them could drive a six inch nail into wood with a blow of his fist. And so, when, at Christmas, 1612, news arrived that the MacNeishes had ambushed and robbed the party bringing seasons provisions to the MacNab stronghold, it was to be expected that some fearful revenge would be planned. Finlay MacNab, though, was for immediate action. The most important supply taken by the MacNeishes was a consignment of good whisky from Perth. The sin was cardinal and the punishment had to fit.

His sons demurred that there was four feet of snow on the ground, a new blizzard blowing and the MacNeish's island castle was ten miles away over rough country with all the boats on Loch Earn tied up in its harbour.

"The night is the night," replied their father implacably, "if the lads are the lads!"

His eldest son, Ian Mir or Smooth Ian, so named for his skill in making executions swift rather than his suavity of manner, soon worked out a plan. The strongest sons would take their own boat on their shoulders to Loch Earn and there surprise the robbers who were no doubt already drunk on their booty.

This proposal would have been formidable even in the best of weather but at midnight on a frozen Christmas it seemed sheer madness. But the MacNabs had to choose between the snowy night and an angry father and so were soon trooping off down to Loch Tay to fetch their boat for their journey.

They reached Loch Earn at four in the morning and spied on the MacNeishes' drunken revelry from the bank. Moving silently out to the island, the MacNabs sunk all their enemies' boats and crept up to the castle door. The MacNeishes, their safety seemingly guaranteed by the wildness of the night and the isolation of their island, had carelessly left the castle open and unguarded and so the first they knew of their peril was when three fatal knocks reverberated on the door of their hall, instantly plunging their carouse into a shivering silence.

Two battle axes came through the hall door, followed by four MacNabs whose dirks and swords were soon flashing into their enemies' flesh.

Only two MacNeishes survived, one hidden under an upturned cot while a young boy jumped from a window. As the MacNabs were leaving, they realised that their father would required some proof of their success and so, lifting one of the sacks which had carried the stolen provisions, Smooth Ian went round the hall, filling it with the heads of the dead. And now it was back to Loch Tay where 10 neatly severed MacNeish heads were deposited at their father's feet.

*Chapter four:*

# The mightiest MacNab!

**In 1654, the ancient MacNab fortress on the River Lochy was stormed and burned to the ground by the Campbells who were, as usual, taking advantage of their neighbours' misfortunes. Once again, the MacNabs were at a low point. Their chief was a 14-year-old boy without a home, with much of his land confiscated and with many of his men lying dead on a dozen fields in Scotland and England.**

Probably because of this experience, the family was quiet during the Jacobite Rebellions of 1689 and 1715, though many of the clansmen fought for the Old Cause at Sheriffmuir and Killiecrankie. At the time of the '45, the chief had two sons in the Black Watch and was firmly pro-Government. His eldest son, John, was captured by the Jacobites at Prestonpans and imprisoned for the duration of the Rebellion in Doune Castle. Later he had a more successful career in Canada and his services in the Whig cause secured him a good deal of the land of forfeited neighbours.

Unfortunately, he produced a son who was to drink, gamble and womanise his way through the whole family fortune – Francis, the MacNab who had 32 illegitimate children, drank whisky by the gallon and greeted an Edinburgh tourist with, "The Highlands are no place for a man with breeches on!"

It was the times that made MacNab. Early on he realised that his income could not cope with his extravagant tastes but that there was an indefinite number of Lowlanders sufficiently impressed by his swaggering air and dramatic title to give him almost endless credit. Those who dared to demand payment of bills signed 'The MacNab' could always be scared off by one of his frightening outbursts of rage. The MacNab in one of these attitudes was indeed a fearful prospect.

One creditor was seen by MacNab coming up the drive one evening. The Chief withdrew to a hiding place and gave orders that the visitor should be given as much whisky as he could swallow and told that the Laird would be back in the morning. The bailiff, a rather prim Edinburgh gentleman, refused to discuss his business with anyone but the Chief himself and at first refused the refreshments. In time, though, he was persuaded to sample the famed MacNab liquor and soon succumbed to its charms. Next morning he woke with a splitting headache and a definite sense of unease, confirmed to the full when he looked out of his window and saw a city-clad gentleman, not unlike himself, swinging by the neck from one of the nearby trees. Trembling into his clothes, he bolted downstairs and asked for an explanation of the frightful spectacle.

"Oh, that's just a wee bit baillie body who asked the MacNab for payment of bills, sir," replied the chief's steward. "Now will you no' tell us whit your ain business is, sir, for the MacNab is due back soon."

Needless to say, the poor man was soon hurrying down the driveway, reducing the family to tears of laughter as they took down the dummy from the tree.

The tallest stories concern the MacNab's drinking feats. He imbibed from a nine gallon jug called 'The Bachelor', handed down in the family for many generations and filled only with a super brew produced by his own illicit still, as one contemporary put it, "He was an imminent Bacchanalian, a man scarce to be seen again!"

He contented himself with the girls of his estate, none of whom was safe from him and several of whom were said to have contracted 'the bad disorder' by submitting to his intentions. One day he saw two boys with his own red hair fighting furiously in the main street of Killin. As the mothers came out to separate them, the MacNab asked the boys why they were fighting. "I said I was the Chief's son," relied the first, "and he said he was."

"Ah, boys, dinnae fight over that," said MacNab, winking at the mothers. "Ye both are."

*Chapter five:*

# Rebellion and scandal

**The MacNab eventually died as he had lived in
1816, cursing the doctors for forbidding him
drink and surrounded by rumours of a secret
marriage and son, probably spread by those
anxious to prevent the succession of his sinister
nephew Alexander.**

But the latter did succeed to debts of
£35,000 and an income of £100 per annum and
sullied the MacNab name by his attempts to make
up the difference.

Alexander was as proud and as extravagant as his uncle but crueller and more self centred, vices which he probably picked up as an
apprentice barrister and man-about-town in
London and Paris where he had already hocked
his uncle's title as a means of gaining credit and
was now determined to hock his own.

But what worked for Francis, who in all
probability just did not understand finance, was

transparent fraud in Alexander and in 1820 the creditors moved in, led by the Earl of Breadalbane who, in Campbell fashion, had bought up most of the MacNab debts and was now in a position to realise his family's old ambition of acquiring Glen Dochart.

One stormy evening in the middle of winter Alexander heard that Breadalbane had sent troops to serve an arrestment for debt on him. Seething with humiliation and rage, he fled his home, deserting his clan wife and daughter in a way unparalleled in Highland history. Soon he was sailing for Canada where he had heard there was much land to be had and many impressionable officials to be galled into parting with it. His reception could not have been more gratifying.

He was given a grant of 80,000 acres and a commission to recruit more of his clansmen from Scotland to work it. It was a testimony to Highland loyalty that, in spite of his recent desertion of them, more than 30 families signed bonds to come out and join him.

However they had a speedy disillusionment. It became clear that Alexander's plan was simply to make as much money from them as quickly as possible in an attempt to pay off his debts and repurchase his Perthshire estates.

MacNab became a tyrant, forcing his men to work in his timber yards when they had a hard enough struggle just surviving in what was still a wilderness and forbidding all projects which might have helped them escape his control.

Then in 1837 the more democratically inclined Canadians rebelled against the corrupt administration which had favoured men like Alexander MacNab.

The Chief himself tried to raise a regiment to combat the rebels but the plan backfired when his men addressed a petition to the Governor saying they would serve under any commander but their own chief.

Once the rebellion was over, a flood of lawsuits came in against Alexander MacNab. In 1848 he returned to Scotland a broke and aged man.

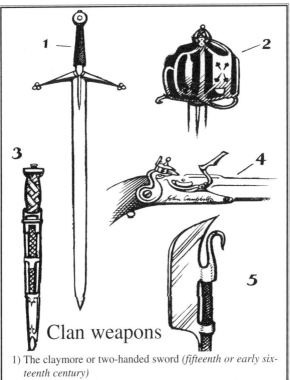

## Clan weapons

1) The claymore or two-handed sword *(fifteenth or early six-teenth century)*
2) Basket hilt of broadsword made in Stirling, 1716
3) Highland dirk *(eighteenth century)*
4) Steel pistol *(detail)* made in Doune
5) Head of Lochaber Axe as carried in the '45 and earlier